Amazing Animals
Hippopotamuses

Please visit our web site at www.garethstevens.com
For a free catalog describing our list of high-quality books, call 1-800-542-2595 (USA) or 1-800-387-3178 (Canada).
Our fax: 1-877-542-2596

Library of Congress Cataloging-in-Publication Data

Wilsdon, Christina.
    Hippopotamuses / by Christina Wilsdon.
         p. cm. — (Amazing animals)
      Originally published: Pleasantville, NY : Reader's Digest Young Families, c2006.
      Includes bibliographical references and index.
      ISBN-10: 0-8368-9119-8   ISBN-13: 978-0-8368-9119-5 (lib. bdg.)
      ISBN-10: 1-4339-2123-5   ISBN-13: 978-1-4339-2123-0 (soft cover)
  1. Hippopotamus—Juvenile literature. I. Title.
  QL737.U57W56 2009
  599.63'5—dc22   2009003828

This edition first published in 2010 by
Gareth Stevens Publishing
A Weekly Reader® Company
1 Reader's Digest Road
Pleasantville, NY 10570-7000 USA

This edition copyright © 2010 by Gareth Stevens, Inc. Original edition copyright © 2006 by Reader's Digest Young Families, Pleasantville, NY 10570

Executive Managing Editor: Lisa M. Herrington
Senior Editor: Brian Fitzgerald
Senior Designer: Keith Plechaty

Produced by Editorial Directions, Inc.
Art Direction and Page Production: The Design Lab/Kathleen Petelinsek and Gregory Lindholm

Consultant: Robert E. Budliger (Retired), NY State Department of Environmental Conservation

Photo Credits
Front cover: Corel Corporation; title page: Shutterstock, Inc./Todd Hackwelder; contents: Shutterstock, Inc./Johan Swanepoel; pages 6–7: IT Stock; page 8: Shutterstock, Inc./Jiri Cvrk; page 11: IT Stock; page 12: Brand X Pictures; pages 14–15: Shutterstock, Inc./N Joy Neish; page 16: Dynamic Graphics, Inc.; page 18: Brand X Pictures; page 19: Shutterstock, Inc./Johan Swanepoel; page 20: Image Source; pages 22–23: Shutterstock, Inc./Kondrachov Vladimir; page 24: Brand X Pictures; page 27: IT Stock; page 28: Image 100 Ltd.; pages 30–31: ImageState; page 32: Brand X Pictures; page 34: Brand X Pictures; page 35: Image Source; page 36: ImageState; pages 38–39: Shutterstock, Inc./Boleslaw Kubica; page 40 (main): Shutterstock, Inc./Mark Atkins; page 40 (inset): Shutterstock, Inc./Julie Simpson; page 43: Shutterstock, Inc./Pichugin Dmitry; pages 44–45: IT Stock; page 46: Brand X Pictures; back cover: Shutterstock, Inc./Todd Hackwelder.

Every effort has been made to trace the copyright holders for the photos used in this book, and the publisher apologizes in advance for any unintentional omissions. We would be pleased to insert the appropriate acknowledgments in any subsequent edition of this publication.

Printed in the United States of America

1 2 3 4 5 6 7 8 9 14 13 12 11 10 09

Amazing Animals
Hippopotamuses

By Christina Wilsdon

Gareth Stevens
Publishing

Contents

Chapter 1
A Hippo Story

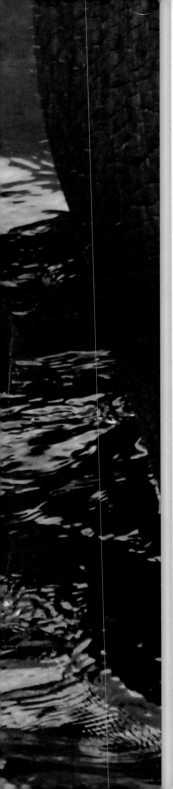

Two big round nostrils poke out of the muddy water of an African lake. Water sprays as a loud snort bursts from them. These nostrils belong to a river hippopotamus that has come up to take a breath.

Suddenly, a smaller pair of nostrils pops up nearby. They open and suck in air. These nostrils belong to a baby hippo that has just been born. This is his very first breath.

The hippo **calf** is only a few minutes old, but he can already walk and swim. He follows his mother to shore on wobbly legs. She turns her enormous head to check on him. No wild animals would dare to attack her, but a hungry crocodile, hyena, or lion might try to catch her calf. If one of these **predators** comes near, the mother hippo will stand like a wall between it and her baby. Or she may charge at the predator and trample it!

Now the mother stops so the baby hippo can drink some milk. As the baby nurses, his nostrils shut and he holds his breath. The calf does not even think about doing this—it just happens automatically. This kind of automatic action is called a **reflex.** Hippo calves have this reflex because they often nurse underwater, where they must hold their breath for up to two minutes.

The baby hippo rapidly grows bigger and stronger. He gains as much as 10 pounds (5 kilograms) a day!

When the baby is almost three weeks old, his mother brings him to the herd. For the first time, he meets other hippo calves and **cows**. There are about 30 hippos altogether, lolling in the mud and snoozing in the water.

Now the mother can leave the baby's side for part of the day. He is old enough to join a "play group" of other calves while his mother takes a break to eat or nap. This group is called a **crèche** (KRESH). The crèche is carefully watched over by a few cows from the herd. These babysitter cows are called **aunts**.

The baby hippo quickly learns that other calves make great playmates. He tussles with the male calves, opening his mouth wide and biting at them. He plays hide-and-seek with the female calves. All the calves shove and push against one another like puppies. They splash and roll in the water.

As the calves play, the aunts stand guard, alert for lions and crocodiles. They also carefully watch any **bull** hippos that come close to the crèche. If the bulls behave too roughly, the cows chase them away.

Fast Facts

A hippo calf weighs 60 to 100 pounds (27 to 45 kg) when it is born. It is about 3 feet (90 centimeters) long and 1½ feet (45 cm) high—just about the size of a potbellied pig.

What's in a Name?

The word *hippo* means "horse" in Greek. The word *hippopotamus* is made up of two Greek words that, when put together, mean "river horse." Hippos are not closely related to horses, though. For a long time, people thought hippos were cousins of pigs. Now scientists have learned that hippos are most closely related to another **mammal** that lives in the water: the whale.

By the time the baby hippo is six months old, he weighs a whopping 500 pounds (227 kg). However, he is still small enough to climb onto the mother's back as she rests in the water. Sometimes he dozes on top of her. Other times he uses her as a diving platform, climbing up one side and flopping back into the water on the other.

The mother hippo nuzzles her baby as she grooms him. She also teaches him proper hippo behavior. If he misbehaves, she bumps him with her head, nips him, or even knocks him down.

The baby hippo begins to **graze** on grass in addition to drinking his mother's milk. Soon he will be weaned, which means he will no longer nurse from his mother. When he is eight months old, he will eat only grass and plants.

When the baby is one year old, he is old enough to live on his own. Some male one-year-olds leave the herd, waiting for the day they can claim a patch of river to make their own. The female calves, however, stay with the herd. They will have their first calves when they are about seven years old.

For now, the baby is content to remain with the herd. A young hippo may tag after its mother until he is four years old, when he is fully grown.

Chapter 2

The Body of a Hippo

A hippo sleeping in water automatically rises to the surface every few minutes for a breath of fresh air. Then it slowly sinks again.

Like a Tank

The hippopotamus is the world's third-largest land animal. It can measure up to 15 feet (457 centimeters) long, about the length of a minivan. It can weigh about 6,000 pounds (2,722 kg). Some very big males weigh in at 8,000 pounds (3,629 kg). The only other land animals that are bigger are the elephant and the white rhinoceros. All three of these giant mammals live in Africa.

Four short, thick legs hold up a hippo's barrel-shaped body. Each foot has four toes linked by stretchy flaps of skin. When a hippo walks, the toes spread apart and help it plod across muddy ground. In the water, these flaps help it swim, just as a duck's webbed feet help it paddle.

A hippo may seem slow and sleepy. However, on land a hippo can trot as fast as a person can run. It can gallop nearly as fast as a horse for a short distance. It does not veer around things. Like a tank, it crashes through them—or over them!

Take a Deep Breath!

A hippo usually stays underwater for up to five minutes. Some people say a hippo can hold its breath for up to 30 minutes.

A hippo's weight allows it to walk underwater, right on the bottom of lakes and rivers. A hippo can even leap along the bottom in a series of graceful bounds. This motion is called **punting**.

Look and Listen

As big as a hippo is, sometimes only its nostrils are seen. A hippo may stay underwater all day, poking its nostrils out to breathe. Its eyes also sit on top of its head so that the hippo can peek above water while hiding under it. Its ears stick out of the water, too.

When a hippo sinks underwater, it closes its nostrils and folds its ears back against its head. This keeps water out of its ears. Yet the hippo can still hear underwater. Sound waves travel through a pad of fat in the hippo's lower jaw, then up through the jawbones. From there, the sound waves go to the hippo's ears, which are much like a whale's ears inside. A hippo can even tell what direction an underwater sound is coming from by comparing what it "hears" on the left and right sides of its jaw.

Heavy Head

A hippo's head weighs nearly 1,000 pounds (454 kg)—about as much as a horse. Its head makes up about one-third of the hippo's length.

A hippo can hear both above the water and under the water at the same time. Above the water, it listens with its ears. Under the water, it picks up sounds with its jaws.

A hippo's tusks can grow to be 30 inches (76 cm) long. You can see only part of a tusk because most of it is buried in the jaw.

Open Wide!

A hippo's head is mostly mouth. When the hippo yawns, its mouth stretches 4 feet (122 cm) wide.

Inside the mouth are as many as 44 teeth. In front, four large teeth called tusks stick out from the top and bottom jaws. In between the tusks are pointed front teeth called incisors. Tusks and incisors grow throughout the hippo's life. Every time the hippo opens and shuts its mouth, the top and bottom tusks and incisors rub against one another. This rubbing keeps them from getting too long. It also keeps them sharp, so they can be used as weapons.

A hippo gathers food with its lips. It clamps them around tufts of grass, then swings its head to rip off the blades. Its large tongue shovels the food to the back of its mouth.

Skin Deep

A hippo may look like an armored tank, but its skin is really quite tender. Its only hair consists of some bristles on its ears, snout, and tail. So a hippo gets sunburned easily. Keeping moist is the hippo's only protection against the hot African sun. It wallows in the mud and stays underwater during the day. A hippo's skin also oozes a pinkish, oily liquid that helps keep its skin moist. The liquid works as a sunscreen and seems to kill germs, too.

Chapter 3
A Herd of Hippos

These peaceful-looking cows can become very aggressive if they think their calves are threatened or in any danger.

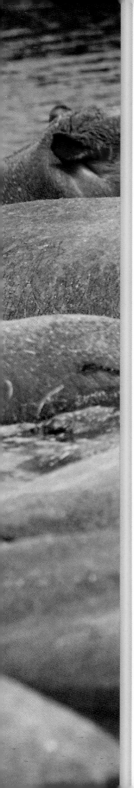

Who's Who?

Rows of big gray boulders stick up out of the water. Egrets and other birds step carefully across them, looking for insects. Suddenly the birds take flight as the boulders move. The boulders are really the round backs of hippos, snoozing the day away.

A hippo herd ranges in size from five hippos to nearly a hundred. It is made up of cows and their calves. The calves include newborns as well as their older sisters. Male calves usually leave the herd after they turn one, but sometimes they stay longer.

Each herd has its own place along the riverbank. Cows chase away cows from another herd if they get too close. They chase away bulls, too. Powerful, **dominant** bulls stake out parts of the riverbank as their own. These areas are called **territories**. A bull defends his territory against other bulls.

Cows and Bulls

Sometimes bulls and cows wrestle with each other in the water. They open their mouths wide and clatter their tusks together. But they are not fighting. All this splashing and clacking is part of hippo **courtship**. A cow and a dominant bull play with each other in this way before mating. The cow gives birth to her calf about eight months later.

Hippo Talk

Hippopotamuses live in water that is thick with mud and muck. It is hard to see in it. But hippos do not need to use their eyesight to find out where other hippos are. They often use sound instead. Scientists have learned that it's noisy beneath the surface! Hippos underwater make all kinds of sounds: croaks, clicks, squeaks, honks, and groans.

Above the water, hippos are noisy, too. A hippo may poke its nostrils out of the water and snort, blowing "raspberries." Bulls bellow loudly. Often, when a bull bellows, other bulls up and down the river bellow back.

Staking a Claim

Finding and keeping a good territory is a bull's full-time job. A young bull must get a territory before he can mate with cows and become a father. The best territory is right on the riverbank, next to the water. However, these good territories already belong to dominant bulls.

To get a territory like this, a bull must fight a dominant bull. If he wins, he gets the territory and becomes the dominant bull. If he loses, he is lucky to escape with his life.

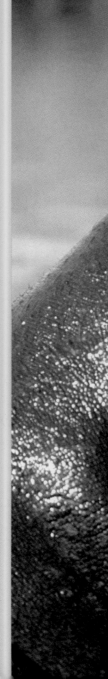

A bull's bellow is very loud. It also makes the air throb! Scientists say hippos can feel a bull's bellow as well as hear it.

Don't You Dare!

A bull bellows to let other bulls know that he is guarding his territory—and they had better stay away.

A Toothsome Twosome

Hippos use their teeth for both love and war! Bulls show off their tusks to other bulls. Fighting hippos stab with them. Courting hippos clack each other with them.

Hippos fight fiercely. Most adult hippo bulls are striped with scars from old battle wounds.

Keep Out!

A dominant bull spends a lot of energy defending his territory. The bull's defense begins with marking his territory with his scent, both on land and in water. Just smelling that a bull owns a territory is enough to make some bulls stay away. The bull also bellows to warn off intruders.

If a bull enters his territory anyway, the dominant bull challenges him. First, he yawns widely at the intruder to show off his enormous tusks. The intruder may yawn back at him. Then, the dominant bull snorts and bellows until the intruder leaves or stands and fights.

The two bulls in a fight for territory charge at each other. In the water, each bull uses his lower jaw as a bucket, scooping up water and tossing it at his opponent. The bulls open their mouths wide. They slash at each other with their razor-sharp tusks. They lock teeth and shove each other like two goats locking horns. They snap at each other's front legs. A hippo bull can break another bull's leg if he can get a grip on it.

The fight ends when one bull has had enough—or when one bull is killed. The winner keeps the territory. If the loser survives, he leaves.

Chapter 4
A Hippo's Day

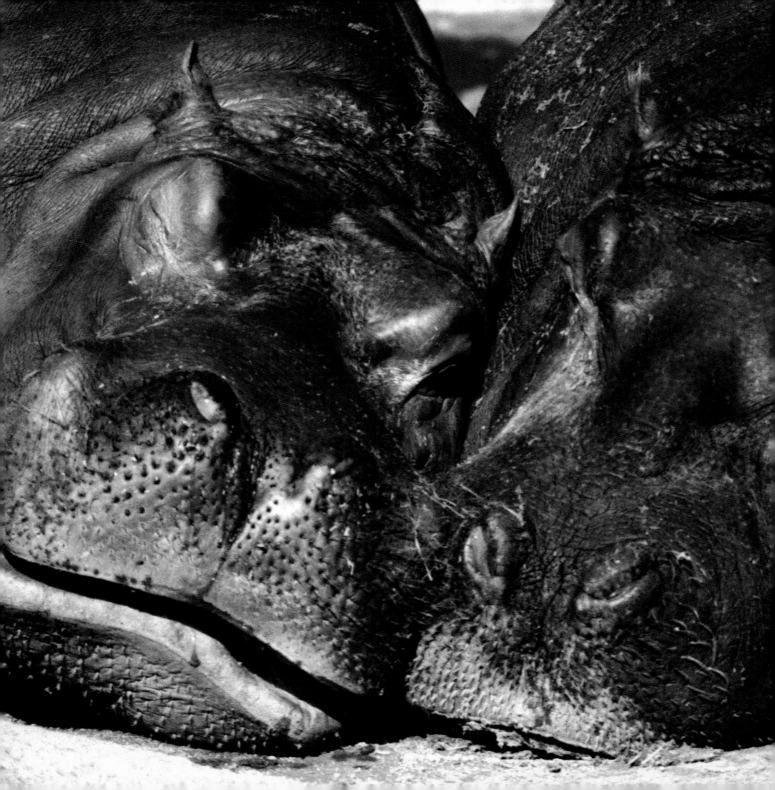

Hippos stay close together during the day. At night, when they leave the mud and water to graze, they go off alone.

Keeping Cool

Hippos spend most of the day lolling in water. Occasionally, they lumber ashore to lie in the sun. That doesn't mean they are lazy. A hippo lacks sweat glands, so it cannot sweat to cool off. If a hippo stays out in the hot sun, its skin starts to dry and crack. The hippo can also overheat and get very thirsty.

So a hippo uses the daytime for sleeping and resting in cool water and mud, safe from the sun's burning rays. The water and mud also help to keep biting insects away.

While the hippo naps, its body is busy digesting the grass and leaves it ate the night before. Grass and leaves are difficult to digest. It may take as long as two days for a single meal to move through the hippo's digestive system.

Waking Up

The sun begins to set, and the hippos begin to stir. The calves play. The cows rumble and click to one another below the water. The hippos trudge out of the water and up the riverbank. It is time to find grass to eat.

Amazing Grazing

The hippos follow well-worn paths to the grazing grounds. These paths have been carved out by the hippos over many years. Along the way, the paths branch out into many other paths. Each cow and calf follows a different one. Hippos spend all day with their herd, but at night they graze alone or with just their young.

Rip, rip, rip goes the grass as hippos swings their heads, using their lips to tear the blades up. Hippos will spend about five hours eating grass and leaves. They will also eat any fruit they find lying on the ground. Hippos may wander from 3 to 6 miles (5 to 10 kilometers) as they graze.

People who live in areas with hippos know that they must be careful if they go out into the wild at night. They do not want to surprise a grazing hippo. Hippos may look a bit silly, but they are actually one of the most dangerous animals in Africa. A frightened hippo will attack humans as well as other animals.

Super-Size Smile!

A hippo's big lips are strong for grazing on grass. A bull's lips can measure 20 inches (51 cm) across.

34

During a single night's grazing, a hippo will eat 100 pounds (45 kg) of food!

Home Sweet Home

The river hippopotamus's name is a clue to its main **habitat**—rivers! Hippos also live in lakes and wetlands. They need deep water sources that do not dry up for part of the year. In times of **drought**, hippos may be forced to wander long distances to find another habitat.

The river hippopotamus is also known as the common hippopotamus and the Nile hippopotamus.

At Home in the Water

As dawn approaches, the hippos return to the river. They slip into the water to nap the hot day away. Their full stomachs slowly get to work digesting their food. If necessary, the hippos can go for two weeks or more without eating. They are so big and use so little energy that they can make their big meals last a long time.

As they wallow in the water, the hippos also help make it a better habitat for other animals that live there. They do this simply by digesting their food and producing droppings. Hippo droppings work as a fertilizer in the water, helping tiny plants grow. It also helps pond scum, or algae, grow well. Fish eat the tiny creatures that feed on the algae and plants. Then birds and crocodiles eat the fish.

Every step a hippo takes in the water helps feed other animals. A hippo is so heavy that it can walk on the bottom of a river or lake. Its feet stir up mud as it moves. Tiny animals in the mud are kicked up, becoming meals for fish.

Fish also nuzzle along the hippos' sides, nibbling on algae that cling to their rough skin. Above the water, egrets and other birds perch on the hippos. They pick off and eat ticks and other pests.

Chapter 5
Hippos in the World

Little Hippo

There are two **species** of hippos: the river hippopotamus and the pygmy hippopotamus. The pygmy hippo lives in forests near swamps and rivers. It is much smaller. It is about 5 feet (152 cm) long and stands about 3 feet (91 cm) tall. It weighs about 500 pounds (227 kg)— less than a river hippo's head!

Where Hippos Live

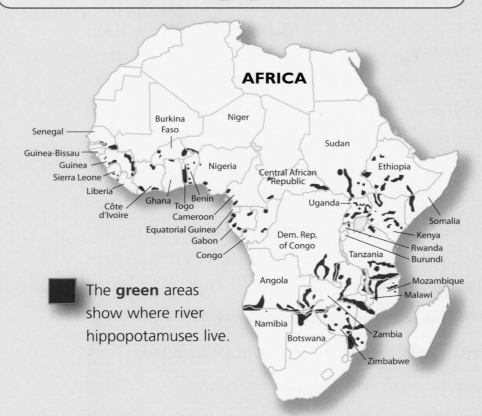

AFRICA

Senegal
Guinea-Bissau
Guinea
Sierra Leone
Liberia
Côte d'Ivoire
Ghana
Togo
Benin
Cameroon
Equatorial Guinea
Gabon
Congo
Burkina Faso
Niger
Nigeria
Central African Republic
Sudan
Ethiopia
Uganda
Somalia
Kenya
Rwanda
Burundi
Dem. Rep. of Congo
Tanzania
Mozambique
Malawi
Angola
Namibia
Botswana
Zambia
Zimbabwe

The **green** areas show where river hippopotamuses live.

Thousands of years ago, river hippopotamuses lived throughout Africa. They were common in the Nile River of Egypt. The ancient Egyptians feared and respected them.

Hunting by humans, however, caused the disappearance of hippos from northern Africa and parts of western Africa. The spread of deserts and the growth of farms and cities have also made hippo habitats shrink. Today, scientists estimate that there are about 157,000 hippos. Their **range** is mainly in East Africa and southern Africa. About 2,000 pygmy hippos survive in Liberia and a few other African countries.

41

The Future of Hippos

Hippos have long been hunted by humans for food. But in the 1700s, European explorers began hunting hippos for sport. By the early 1800s, the thousands of hippos that lived along Egypt's Nile River were all gone. Today, hippos are most threatened by people hunting them illegally for tusks and meat.

Habitat loss is another threat facing hippos. Hippos need room to roam and graze. They also require water. The growing human population is using more and more hippo habitat for farms and towns. Rice paddies are replacing wetlands. Angry farmers sometimes kill hippos that eat their crops.

Fast Facts About River Hippopotamuses

Scientific name	*Hippopotamus amphibius*
Class	Mammals
Order	Artiodactyla
Size	Males: up to 15 feet (457 cm) long Females: up to 14 feet (427 cm) long
Weight	Males: to 8,000 pounds (3,629 kg) Females: to 5,100 pounds (2,313 kg)
Life span	Up to 40 years in the wild
Habitat	Rivers, lakes, wetlands
Top speed	About 30 miles (48 km) per hour

Hippo Fish Farmers!

Hippo droppings fertilize plants in the water and help provide food for fish. The capturing of hippos around one African lake caused its fish populations to decrease. This is creating problems for people who live in the area and make their living by fishing.

Glossary

aunt—a hippo cow that babysits the calves of other cows

bull—an adult male hippo

calf—a baby hippo

courtship—the behavior used by male and female hippos to pair up as mates

cow—an adult female hippo

crèche—a group of hippo calves

dominant—describing the most powerful or strongest hippo in a group

drought—a long period of time without rain

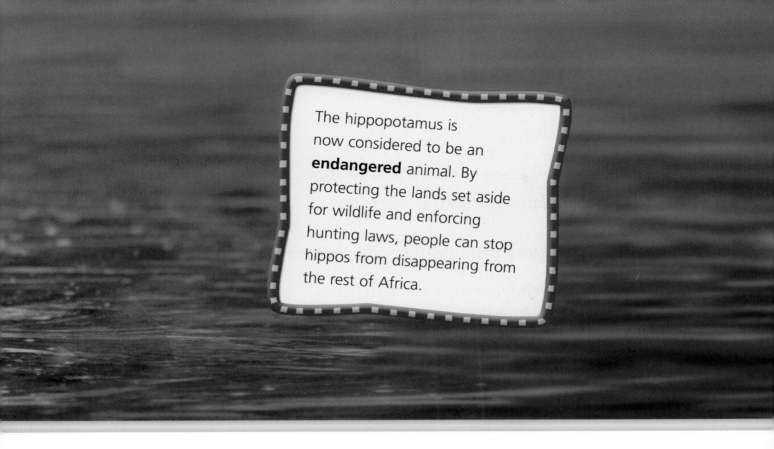

The hippopotamus is now considered to be an **endangered** animal. By protecting the lands set aside for wildlife and enforcing hunting laws, people can stop hippos from disappearing from the rest of Africa.

endangered—at risk of dying out

graze—to feed on grass

habitat—the natural environment where an animal or plant lives

mammal—a kind of animal with a backbone and hair on its body; it drinks milk from its mother when it is born

predator—an animal that hunts and eats other animals to survive

punting—the motion a hippo uses to leap along in the water

range—all the places where a species lives

reflex—an automatic action

species—a group of living things that are the same in many ways

territory—an area that an animal considers to be its own and will fight to defend

Hippos: Show What You Know

How much have you learned about hippos? Grab a piece of paper and a pencil and write your answers down.

1. Why do baby hippos close their nostrils and hold their breath when drinking milk?

2. What does the word *hippopotamus* mean in Greek?

3. How long can a hippo hold its breath?

4. How much does the head of a fully grown hippo weigh?

5. How do hippos find each other under the muddy water?

6. What kinds of hippos live in a herd?

7. Why do hippos spend most of the day in the water?

8. How long does it take for a hippo to digest a meal?

9. What caused the disappearance of hippos from parts of Africa?

10. How many hippos are there in the world today?

9. Hunting by humans 10. About 157,000
4. Nearly 1,000 pounds (454 kg) 5. By using sounds 6. Cows and calves 7. Their skin is very sensitive to the sun and they lack sweat glands to help them cool off. 8. Up to two days
1. It is a reflex, because they often nurse underwater. 2. River horse 3. Up to 30 minutes

For More Information

Books

Allen, Christina. *Hippos in the Night: Autobiographical Adventures in Africa*. New York: HarperCollins Publishers, 2003.

Feldhake, Glenn. *Hippos: Natural History & Conservation* (WorldLife Library). St. Paul: Voyageur Press, 2005.

Haas, Robert B. *African Critters*. Washington, DC: National Geographic Children's Books, 2008.

Web Sites

Animal Planet: Hippopotamus

http://animal.discovery.com/mammals/hippopotamus/

Learn interesting details, watch videos, and take a quiz to test your knowledge of hippos.

National Geographic Kids: Hippopotamuses

http://kids.nationalgeographic.com/Animals/CreatureFeature/Hippopotamus

Get quick facts, print out images, and see photos of hippos.

Publisher's note to educators and parents: Our editors have carefully reviewed these web sites to ensure that they are suitable for children. Many web sites change frequently, however, and we cannot guarantee that a site's future contents will continue to meet our high standards of quality and educational value. Be advised that children should be closely supervised whenever they access the Internet.

Index